Rose Dream Origami

Toshikazu Kawasaki

Asahi Press

A complete guide to six types of Kawasaki Rose,
supplemented by online videos showing the models being folded by the author

This edition published by Asahi Press
3-3-5 Nishikanda, Chiyoda-ku, Tokyo 101-0065, Japan
Tel. 81-3-3263-3326 Fax. 81-3-3239-0479
http://www.asahipress.com/

Copyright ©2016 by Toshikazu Kawasaki
ISBN: 978-4-255-00941-4 C0076

All rights reserved. No part of this publication may be reproduced, stored in a retrieval system, or transmitted in any way or by any means, electronic, mechanical, photocopying, recording or otherwise, without the prior written permission of the copyright holder.

Publisher : Masanori Hara
Translation : Marcio Noguchi
Design : Pool Graphics
Photography : Hirotaka Yonekura
Origami paper : Ehime Shiko Co., Ltd.
Support : Tohan Corporation(Honwoueru Project)

Introduction

Compiled 30 years after the birth of the Kawasaki Rose, this book brings together the instructions for six types of origami rose in a single volume. The folding sequences have been improved, and the diagrams have been redrawn to make them clearer and easier to understand. I have also made available online videos showing models being folded by my own hands.

The first two models, the "Bud" and "Blossomed Rose", are also known overseas as the "Kawasaki Rose" and are often used as gifts at wedding receptions. The "Kawasaki Rose" is considered a symbol of peace in the city of Fukuyama (Hiroshima Prefecture), much as the origami crane is considered a symbol of the peace in the city of Hiroshima (also in Hiroshima Prefecture). As such, several tens of thousands of Kawasaki Roses are folded every year.

The "1-minute Rose" comes in handy on many occasions. As a gift in appreciation for a nice meal, for example it allows us to become friends with the chef of a restaurant. The "3-minute Rose" is a new variant that can be considered the "bud" version of the "1-minute Rose". With enough practice, you'll be able to fold it in about three minutes, so feel free to use it in a similar way as the "1-minute Rose".

The "Rose Leaf" has been improved too. Making use of the "spiral lock" technique, the old 3-leaflet Leaf has turned into a more realistic 5-leaflet Leaf. I have also prepared a Heptagonal Box that can be used as a gift box. This box makes use of this century's most innovative folding technique, which I call the "helical fold". I am sure you will be impressed with it. There is no doubt that learning the origami techniques presented in this book will help you become the next Origami Rose Master.

Contents

★ The number of stars indicates the difficulty level.

Introduction	3	Using the video	8
How to use this book	6	Paper supplement	10
Symbols and basic folds	7		

Kawasaki Rose

Stage 1 Folding the Bud   13
Stage 2 Folding the Blossomed Rose 20

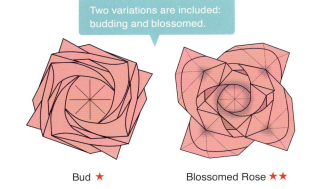

Two variations are included: budding and blossomed.

Bud ★   Blossomed Rose ★★

Rose Leaf

Stage 1 Leaf with 3 Leaflets 25
Stage 2 3-leaflet Module   30
Stage 3 2-leaflet Module   32
Stage 4 Leaf with 5 Leaflets   34

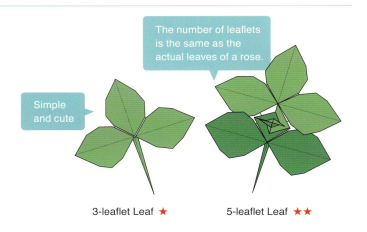

Simple and cute

The number of leaflets is the same as the actual leaves of a rose.

3-leaflet Leaf ★   5-leaflet Leaf ★★

Rosebud 3-minute Rose

Stage 1 Folding the Rosebud   37
Stage 2 Folding the 3-minute Rose   44

Once you get used to it, you can fold this rose in 3 minutes.

Rosebud ★★

Using duo paper, you can fold a rose with a different-colored calyx.

3-minute Rose ★

1-minute Rose

Folding the 1-minute Rose   51

You can devise your own favorite shape by adjusting the references to your taste.

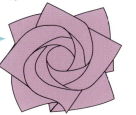

1-minute Rose ★★

Rose

Folding the Rose   59

It is hard to believe it is folded from a single sheet of paper!

Rose ★★★

Heptagonal Rose Box

Stage 1 Heptagonal Box   75
Stage 2 Heptagonal Rose Box   77

Perfect for storing your precious Kawasaki Roses.

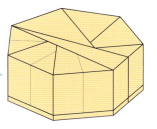

Heptagonal Rose Box ★

How to use this book

Difficulty levels

For each model, the difficulty level is indicated by the number of stars. The more stars, the more challenging it will be.

★ ······ Relatively simple
★★ ······ Not so complex
★★★ ······ Challenging

Types of paper

For each model, an appropriate type of paper is indicated from among five types. A thinner paper is easier to fold, while the thick ones will require more strength. Although construction paper is thicker than Tant, it is also softer.

Thinner → 1 — 2 — 3 — 4 — 5 → Thicker

1. Thin duo paper
2. Regular origami paper
3. Duo paper / Copy paper
4. Tant origami paper
5. Construction paper

Terms in bold

Model names and important terms are printed in bold.

Three tips for neat folding

1 Make the creases sharp

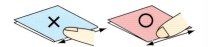

Just creating the creases with the fingers is usually not enough.

Make use of your fingernails or a bone folder to create sharp creases.

2 Be sure to align the edges precisely

Don't let the paper drift and get misaligned. Match the edges as precisely as possible.

3 Check the next step for expected results

By checking the next step, you can see how triangles or layers are supposed to form.

Symbols and basic folds

The following are the symbols used in this book. I suggest you learn their meanings before you start folding.

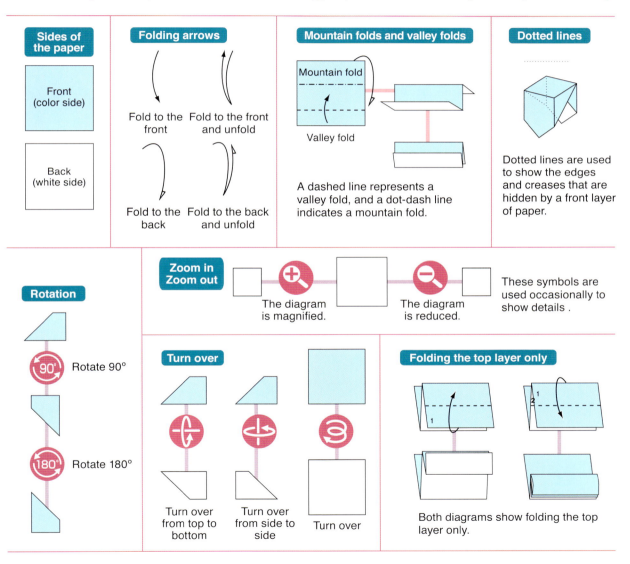

Using the video

In the video, I provide detailed explanations and demonstrate the folding sequences.
I also give hints and tips that would be difficult to provide in a diagram.

Video running time: 140 minutes

How to view the video

If you have purchased this book, you can acquire access to a free commentary video by submitting an application via the URL below. The video is particularly useful for checking the more difficult steps.

http://www.asahipress.com/dgc/roseeg/

Please note that the publisher reserves the right to discontinue the application service or remove the video from the site after three years have elapsed from the time of publication (October 5th, 2016).

About the video

- There are differences from the book in terms of model orientation and folding sequence, to facilitate the recording and commentary.
- In order to clearly differentiate the front from the back, regular origami paper is used (color on one side, white on the other).
- In order to show the creases, a larger paper (24 cm square) is used (except for the Rose Leaf and the Heptagonal Rose Box).

Contents	Page	Step number	Video
Introduction			
Kawasaki Rose			
Stage 1 Folding the Bud	p.13	1	00 : 46
	p.14	18	07 : 14
	p.16	33	11 : 10
	p.17	40	12 : 24
	p.18	49	14 : 50
Stage 2 Folding the Blossomed Rose	p.20	1	21 : 42
	p.20	3 *1	23 : 22
	p.20	3 *2	24 : 45
	p.21	6	25 : 54
Rose Leaf			
Stage 1 Leaf with 3 Leaflets	p.25	1	00 : 46
	p.25	9	04 : 53
	p.28	24	09 : 51

*1 p.17, Step 40   *2 p.18, Step 49

Content		Page	Step number	Video
Stage 2	3-leaflet Module	p.30	1	12 : 35
		p.31	11	15 : 22
		p.31	18	17 : 00
Stage 3	2-leaflet Module	p.32	1	18 : 15
		p.33	10	21 : 19
Stage 4	Leaf with 5 Leaflets	p.34	1	22 : 32
Rosebud / 3-minute Rose				
Stage 1	Folding the Rosebud	p.37	1	01 : 02
		p.38	12	05 : 06
		p.39	23	08 : 04
		p.39	29	11 : 20
		p.40	31	12 : 51
		p.40	36	14 : 42
		p.41	37	15 : 50
		p.42	45	17 : 29
Stage 2	Folding the 3-minute Rose	p.44	1	20 : 37
		p.44	6	22 : 30
		p.45	11	25 : 45
		p.46	18	28 : 09
		p.47	26	30 : 17
1-minute Rose				
Folding the 1-minute Rose		p.51	1	01 : 03
		p.52	12	03 : 05
		p.53	20	04 : 53
		p.55	35	08 : 25
Rose				
Folding the Rose		p.59	1	00 : 48
		p.60	15	04 : 27
		p.61	24	05 : 58
		p.62	27	06 : 46
		p.63	38	10 : 19
		p.66	47	14 : 48
		p.68	54	16 : 20
		p.70	60	20 : 00
Heptagonal Rose Box				
Stage 1	Heptagonal Box	p.75	1	00 : 44
		p.75	9	07 : 12
		p.76	13	10 : 05
Stage 2	Heptagonal Rose Box	p.77	1	11 : 13

Paper supplement

I have specifically selected the accompanying paper so that you can fold beautiful Kawasaki Roses. The recommended paper for each model is provided in a size slightly larger (17.5cm x 17.5cm) than the usual size.

1. Regular origami paper

Recommended for: Kawasaki Rose

Regular origami paper with vibrant colors. Perfect for folding the Kawasaki Rose Bud and the Blossomed Rose.

4 colors (vermilion, sunflower, peach, wisteria) x 2 sheets each

2. Regular origami paper

Recommended for: Rose Leaf

Regular origami paper with vibrant colors. Perfect for folding Rose Leaves.

2 colors (green, viridian) x 3 sheets each

Before you start folding

- The models in this book can be also folded from regular origami paper that is commercially available.
- For the beginners, we recommend practicing with regular paper before using the special paper provided.

Note:
- Paper for the Heptagonal Rose Box is not included.

3. Duo paper

Recommended for: Rosebud

Paper with different colors on front and back. Used in models with color change.

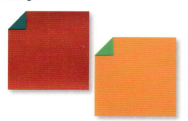

2 color pairs (red/green, yellow-orange/bright green) x 2 sheets each

4. Thin duo paper

Recommended for: Rose

Because this paper is thin, it is slightly more difficult to fold. But it will result in a beautiful model without showing the white from the back of the paper.

2 colors (red, orange) x 2 sheets each

5. Tant origami paper

Recommended for: 1-minute Rose, 3-minute Rose

Tant is a very strong paper that is becoming more commercially available for origami use.

4 colors (N53, N51, N50, N57) x 2 sheets each

折り紙の本・好評発売中!

**使う・遊ぶ
博士の実用夢折り紙**
川崎敏和

B5判並製／136頁／オールカラー
定価(本体1480円+税)

小物入れにぴったりな「箱」シリーズから、ブロック感覚で遊べる「家」まで。楽しいのに、本当に"使える"折り紙が満載!

**折り紙夢WORLD
花と動物編**
川崎敏和

AB判並製／160頁
定価(本体1500円+税)

見れば折りたくなる、きれいで不思議な折り紙。人気の花と動物を、美しいカラー写真とわかりやすい図で紹介。

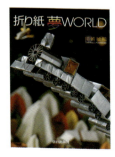

折り紙夢WORLD
川崎敏和

B5判並製／128頁
定価(本体1500円+税)

インテリアやアクセサリーに応用できる、きれいでかわいい折り紙がいっぱい。「銀河鉄道」「バラのブローチ」など、大人から子どもまで幅広く楽しめる内容。

魔法のように立体化する
究極の夢折り紙
川崎敏和

B5判並製／136頁／オールカラー
定価(本体1600円+税)

折り紙博士の最高傑作を集めた折り紙集。コツをつかめば初心者でも折れるので、従来の折り紙では物足りない人や、じっくりと作品作りに取り組んでみたい人におすすめ。

博士の折り紙夢BOOK
川崎敏和

A5判並製／280頁
定価(本体1500円+税)

子どもから大人まで楽しめる夢いっぱいの折り紙144点が一冊に！恐竜、ばら、スペースシャトルなど人気のKawasaki作品および、国内外の名作を収録。

かわいい！かっこいい！美しい！
動物折り紙BOOK
笠原邦彦

B5判並製／128頁／オールカラー
定価(本体1500円+税)

動物や鳥、水の生き物58作品をオールカラーの美しい写真で見せる、絵本感覚の折り紙本。折り紙界の巨匠による、「動物折り紙」の決定版！

朝日出版社 〒101-0065 東京都千代田区西神田3-3-5 TEL 03-3263-3321

Kawasaki Rose

This model was inspired by the roses made of cream that often decorate Christmas cakes in Japan. It was first published in 1985 in *Origami for the Connoisseur* (Japan Publications), and outside of Japan, it has come to be called the "Kawasaki Rose". I introduce two models in the present book. The name "Kawasaki Rose" has since been adopted in Japan too, and now all of my rose variations are known as "Kawasaki Roses".

Difficulty level Bud ★
Blossomed Rose ★★

Kawasaki Rose (Bud)

Stage ▶ 1 Folding the Bud

Recommended paper size: 15 cm - 18 cm square
Paper type: Regular origami paper

1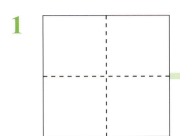
Fold in half, horizontally and vertically.

2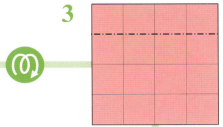
Fold into quarters, edge to the center line. Unfold.

3
Pinch the dot-dash line and make it stand up perpendicularly.

4
Bring the dot-dash edge to the raw edge, creating a valley fold in the middle.

5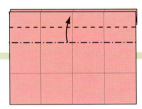
Repeat steps 3 and 4. See the view from the side. Take care to align the paper properly.

× ○
View from the side

6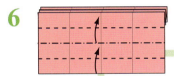
Repeat, creating an **accordion** fold.

7
Unfold completely.

8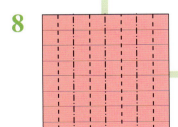
Repeat steps 3 to 7 in the other direction, creating an 8 x 8 grid.

9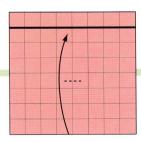
Bring the edge to the thick line, and create a short pinch line using your fingernail.

10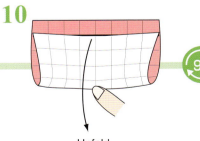
Unfold.

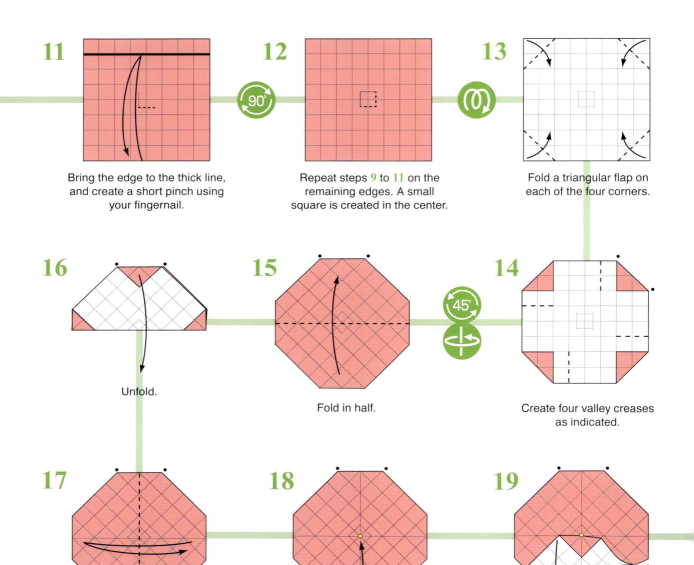

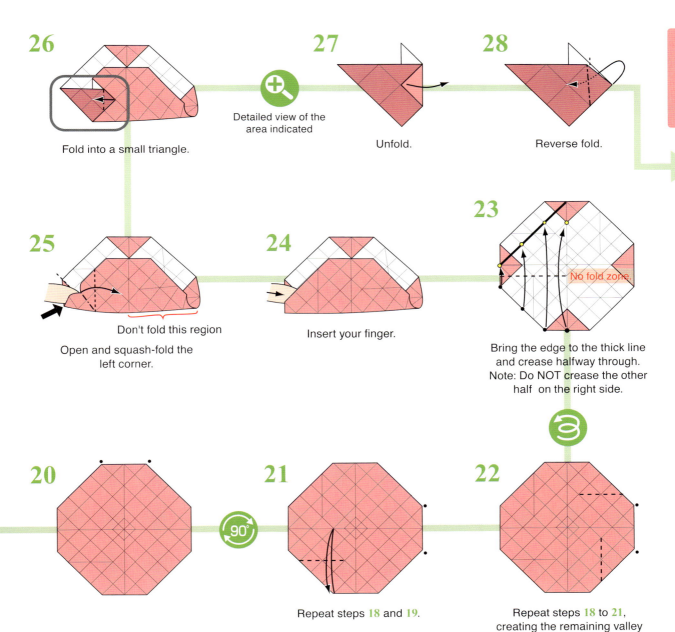

29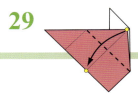
Fold the corner to the point.

30
Zoom out to view the complete model

31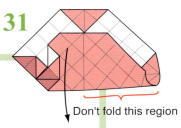
Don't fold this region
Unfold back to step 23.

34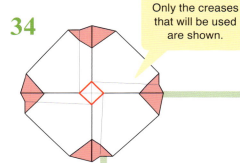
Only the creases that will be used are shown.
Using your finger on the back, flatten the red square.

33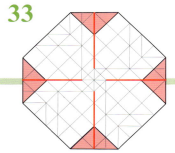
Pinch the red lines, reinforcing them into mountain creases.

32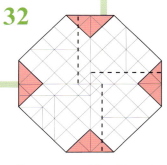
Repeat steps 23 to 31 on the remaining three corners.

35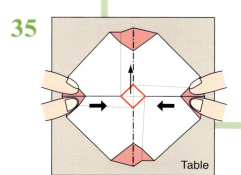
Table
Position the model on top of a table and hold the opposite corners. As you push the flaps towards the center (as indicated by the arrows), the red square in the center should lift up.

36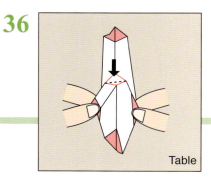
Table
Push the diagonal of the red square.

37
Fold the right flap towards the back and the left flap towards the front, and flatten out the model on the table.

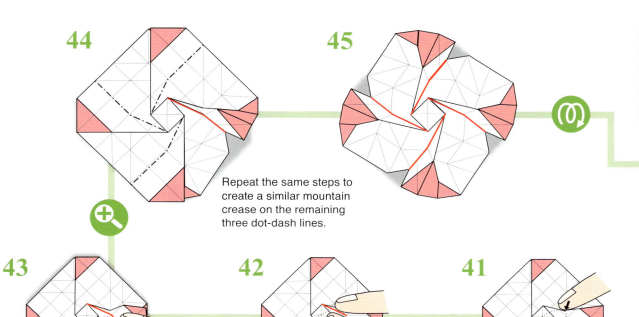

44

45

Repeat the same steps to create a similar mountain crease on the remaining three dot-dash lines.

43

Pushing # from the back, continue pinching to extend the mountain crease indicated in red.

42

Pinch to create a mountain crease as indicated with the red line.

41

Lightly push using your finger in order to flatten the surface as indicated.

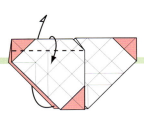

38

Fold down the flap. At the same time, hold the model in the air and open the layer from underneath to the back.

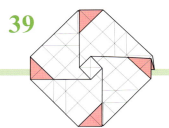

39

40

Insert your finger from the back and position it on the flap indicated with ※.

Kawasaki Rose

17

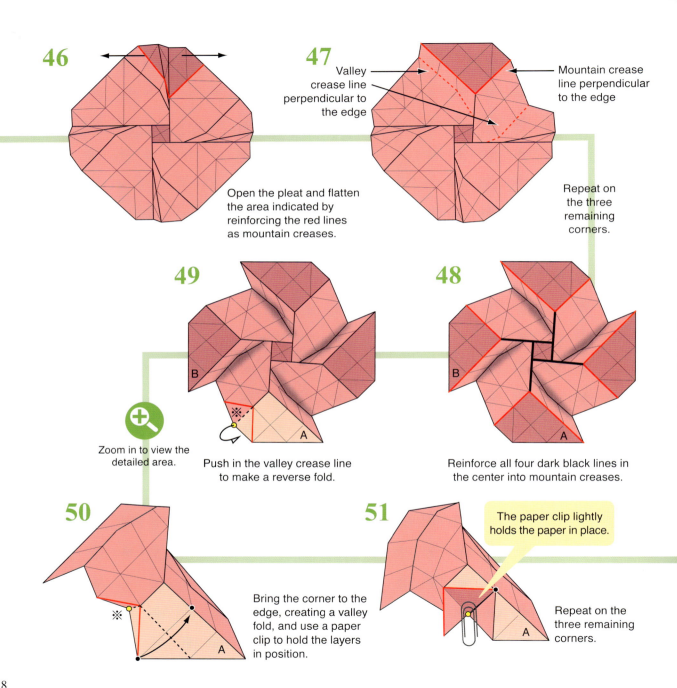

56

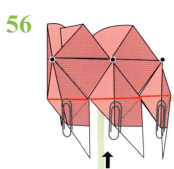

View from the bottom

57

The red dashed line is the red line in step **56** viewed from the bottom.

Fold down the flaps in the order indicated, covering the bottom.

Note
The model will naturally start wrapping around into a three-dimensional shape.

55

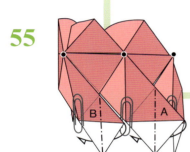

Mountain-fold all four corners.

54

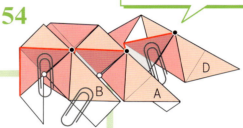

Repeat steps **52** and **53** on the remaining three corners.

52

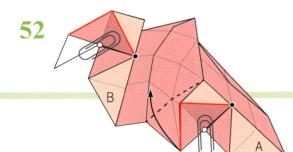

Valley-fold using the existing crease.

53

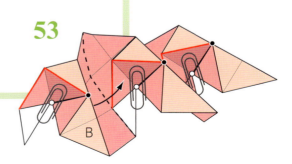

Valley-fold on the dashed line so that B stays on the top layer. Then use the paper clip to lock into position.

58 Insert the last corner inside the pocket ※, locking the base of the model.

59

60 Use a pen or a round tool to better define the curved creases indicated in red.

61 Shape the petals with a light curl.

62 Finished **Bud**

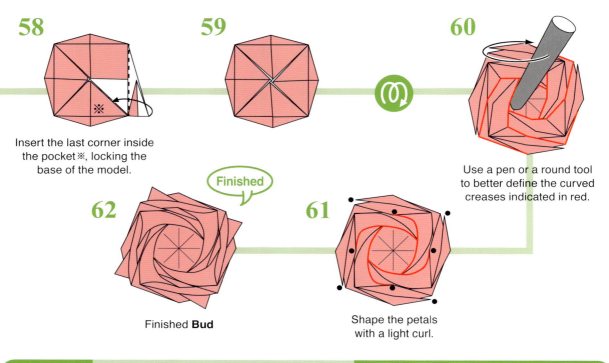

Stage ▶ 2 Folding the Blossomed Rose

Recommended paper size: 15 cm - 18 cm square
Paper type: Regular origami paper

Start with step **33** of the **Bud** Rose.

Only the creases that will be used are shown.

1 Bring the reference points together to create valley creases. Be sure to use your fingernails to create sharp creases.

2 Bring the reference points together to create valley creases. Be sure to use your fingernails to create sharp creases.

3 Similar to **Bud** steps **34** to **54**.

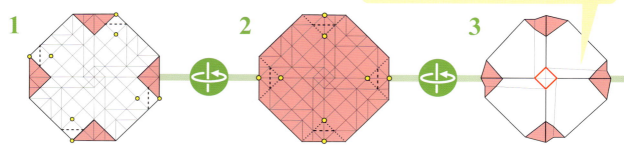

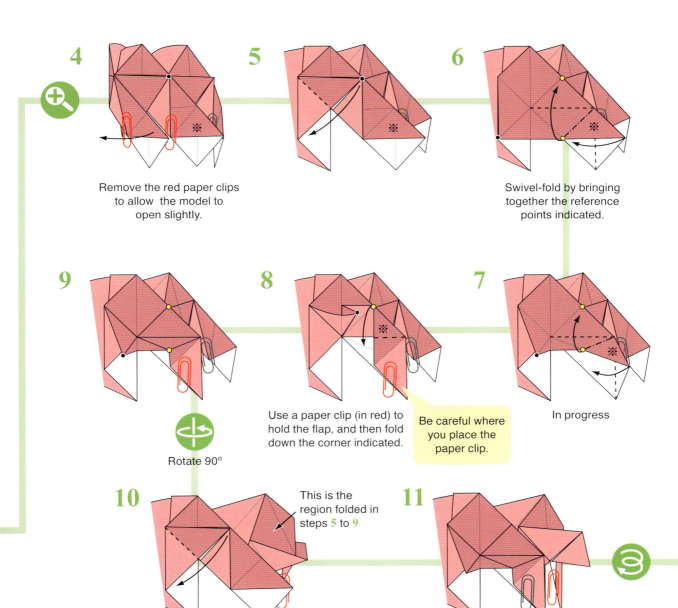

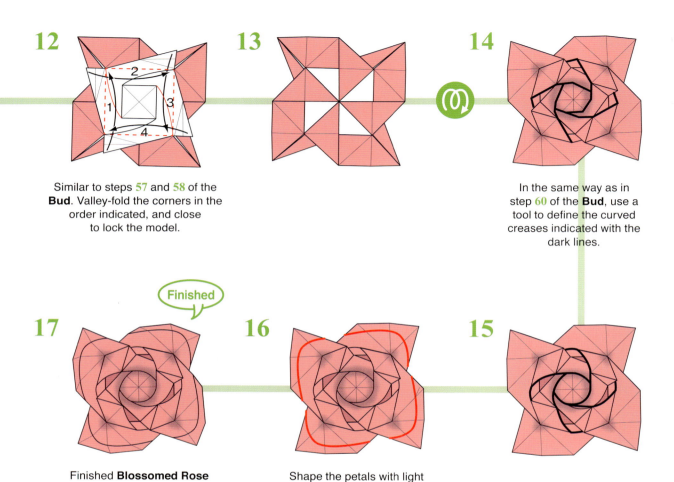

Rose Leaf

In this section, the Leaf with 3 Leaflets and Leaf with 5 Leaflets will be presented. Until recently, only the Leaf with 3 Leaflets was published. But with the use of the "Spiral Lock" mechanism, a more realistic Leaf with 5 Leaflets became possible. Those who find the Leaf with 5 Leaflets challenging can still fold the Leaf with 3 Leaflets with great results.

| Difficulty level | Leaf with 3 Leaflets ★ |
| | Leaf with 5 Leaflets ★★ |

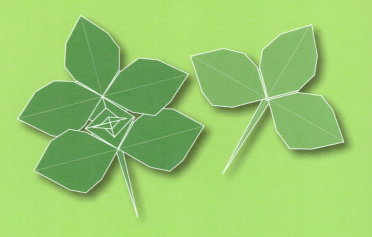

Leaf with 5 Leaflets, Rose

Stage ▶ 1 Leaf with 3 Leaflets

Recommended paper size: 15 cm - 18 cm square
Paper type: Regular origami paper

1

Start with a 4 x 4 grid made of valley creases.

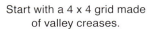

2
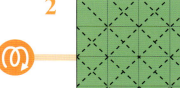
Create the valley crease diagonals indicated.

3
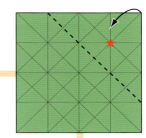
Fold on the dashed line valley crease to make a triangular flap perpendicular to the rest of the paper.

4
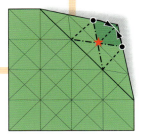
Pushing the red star from the back, bring the points indicated together using the creases indicated.

5
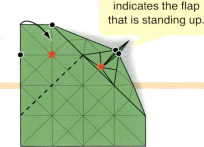
The dark area indicates the flap that is standing up.

Repeat steps 3 to 5 on the top-left corner.

6
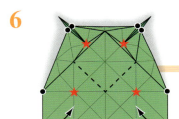
Repeat steps 3 to 5 on the remaining two corners.

7
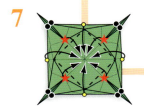
Valley-fold, bringing the corners indicated with the red stars and yellow circles towards the center.

Perspective view

8

Open the triangular flaps to the sides, flattening the model completely.

9

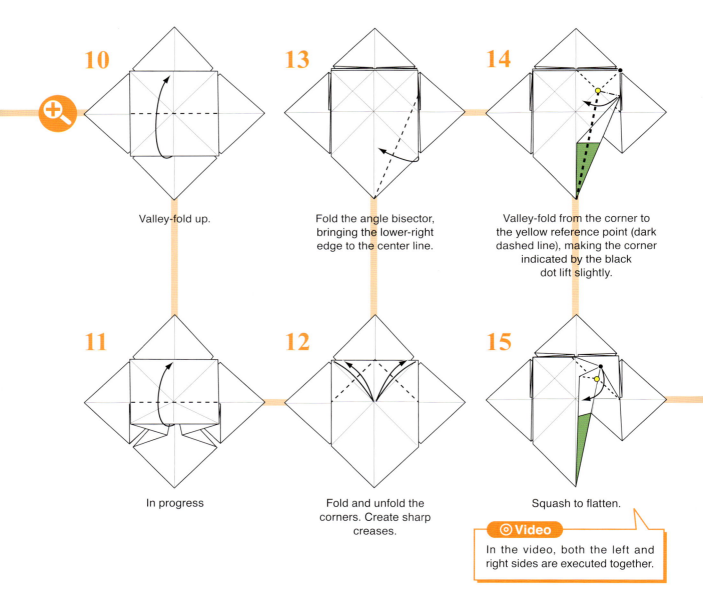

17

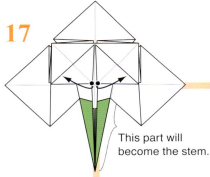

Open slightly.

This part will become the stem.

18

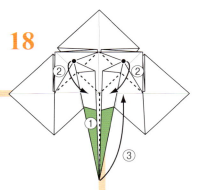

① Valley-fold the stem in half.
② Push down the corners that are slightly open.
③ Fold the stem vertically.

21

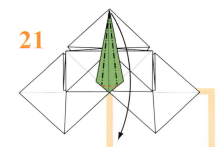

Holding the red dashed line with your fingernail, fold the stem down while mountain-folding the sides to narrow the stem.

Rose Leaf

16

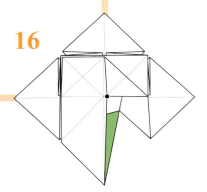

Repeat steps **13** to **16** on the left side.

19

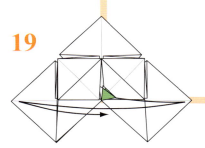

Move the stem to the left and to the right, creating a sharp crease.

20

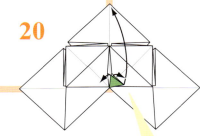

Open and squash the base of the stem, flattening it. See the next step for desired result.

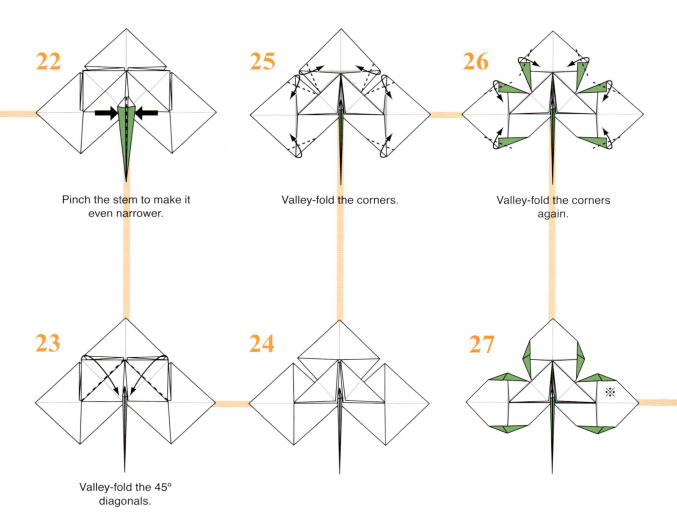

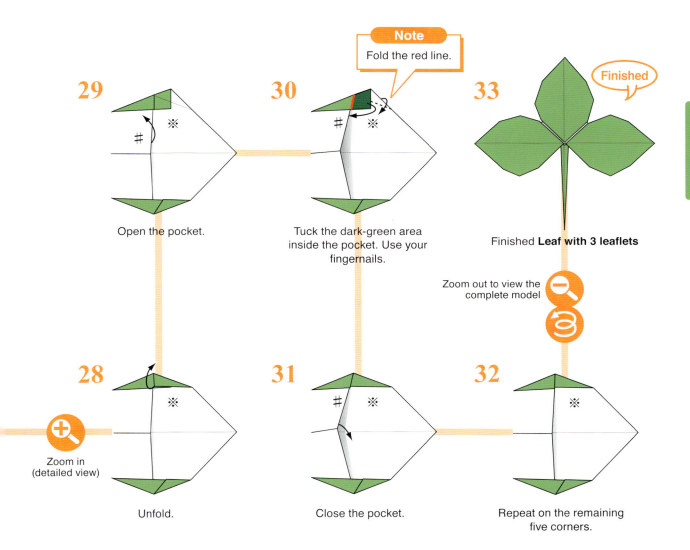

Stage ▶ 2 3-leaflet Module

Recommended paper size: 15 cm - 18 cm square
Paper type: Regular origami paper

This model is created by modifying the stem of the **3-leaflet Leaf** into a "Spiral Lock" connector, which will become one of the modules for the **5-leaflet Leaf**. Start with the **3-leaflet Leaf** folded up to step **12**.

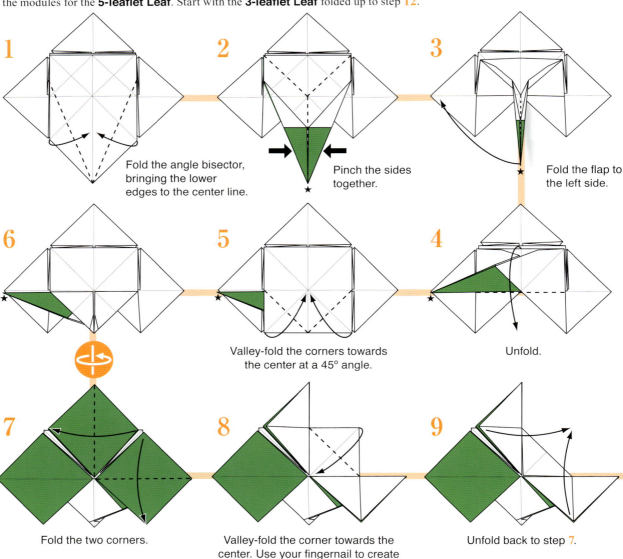

1. Fold the angle bisector, bringing the lower edges to the center line.
2. Pinch the sides together.
3. Fold the flap to the left side.
4. Unfold.
5. Valley-fold the corners towards the center at a 45° angle.
6.
7. Fold the two corners.
8. Valley-fold the corner towards the center. Use your fingernail to create a sharp crease.
9. Unfold back to step **7**.

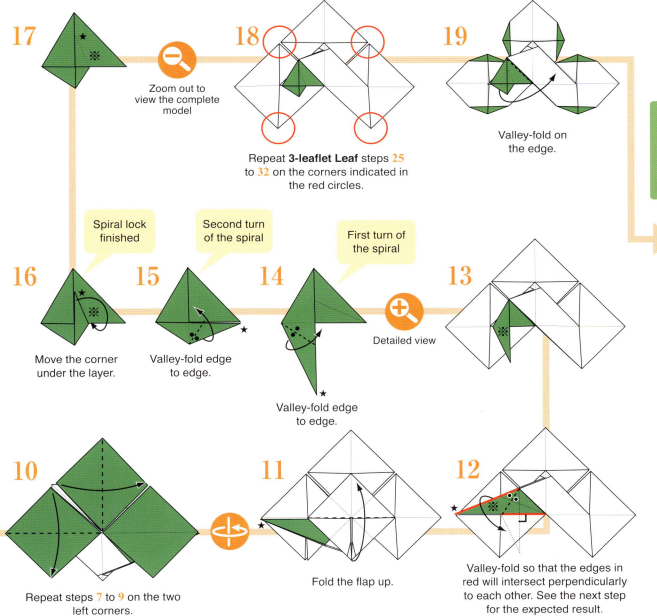

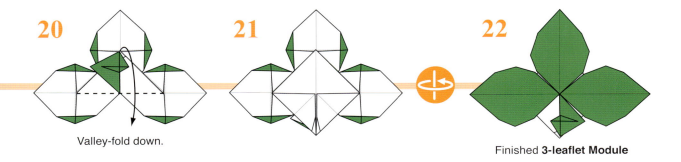

Stage ▶ 3 2-leaflet Module

Recommended paper size: 15 cm - 18 cm square
Paper type: Regular origami paper

Start with the **3-leaflet Leaf** folded up to step **22**. Turn over.

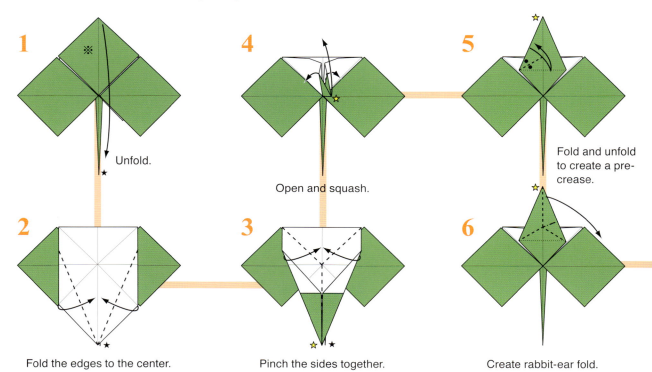

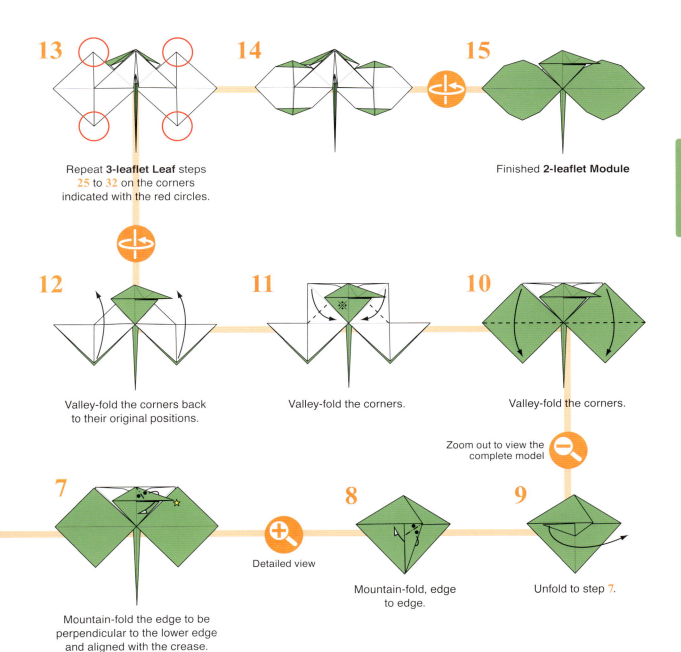

Stage ▶ 4 Leaf with 5 Leaflets

Required: 3-leaflet Module and 2-leaflet Module

Now let's assemble a **5-leaflet Leaf** by connecting the **2-leaflet Module** to the **3-leaflet Module** using the "Spiral Lock" mechanism.

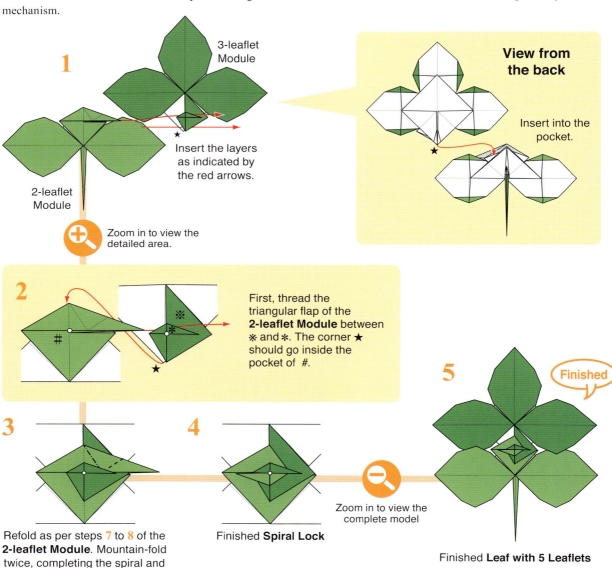

1 3-leaflet Module. 2-leaflet Module. Insert the layers as indicated by the red arrows. Zoom in to view the detailed area.

View from the back — Insert into the pocket.

2 First, thread the triangular flap of the **2-leaflet Module** between ※ and ✱. The corner ★ should go inside the pocket of #.

3 Refold as per steps **7** to **8** of the **2-leaflet Module**. Mountain-fold twice, completing the spiral and locking the model.

4 Finished **Spiral Lock**. Zoom in to view the complete model.

5 Finished. Finished **Leaf with 5 Leaflets**

34

Rosebud / 3-minute Rose

Among the many variations of the rose I created, the Rosebud is one of the oldest and closest to the original. This model involves techniques also used for the Rose: the Three-dimensional Twist Fold and the Three-dimensional Outside Reverse Fold, so be sure to practice those techniques.

The 3-minute Rose is a bud version of the 1-minute Rose, and it is one of the most recent designs among the Kawasaki Rose series.

Difficulty level Rosebud ★★
3-minute Rose ★

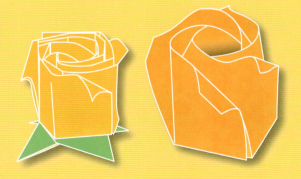

Rosebud, Rose, Leaf with 3 Leaflets

Stage ▶ 1   Folding the Rosebud

Recommended paper size: 15 cm - 18 cm square
Paper type: Duo origami paper

1
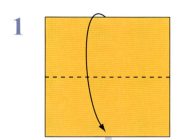
Fold in half.

2
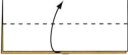
Fold the top layer in half, raw edge to folded edge.

3

Fold the folded edge to the raw edge (both layers of paper).

4
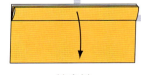
Unfold.

5

Repeat steps **2** to **4** on the other side. Unfold.

6
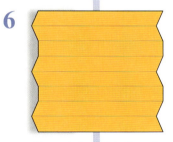
Repeat steps **1** to **5** on the vertical too, creating an 8 x 8 grid. See next step for expected result.

7

8
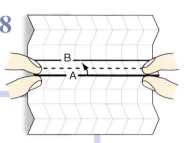
Pinch the dark line A in the center and reinforce the mountain crease. Valley-fold the mountain crease to meet crease B.

9
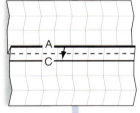
Open line A and bring to line C, creating a valley crease in between.

10
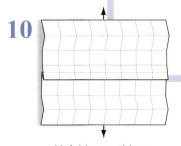
Unfold everything.

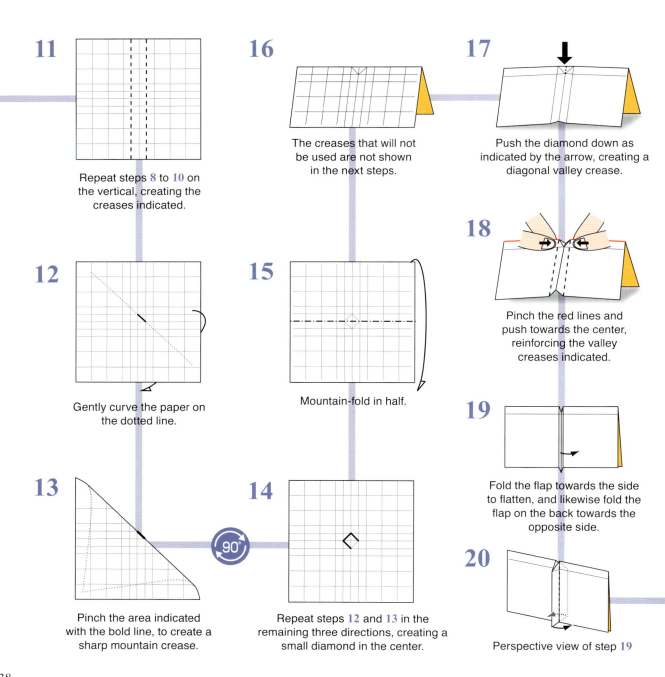

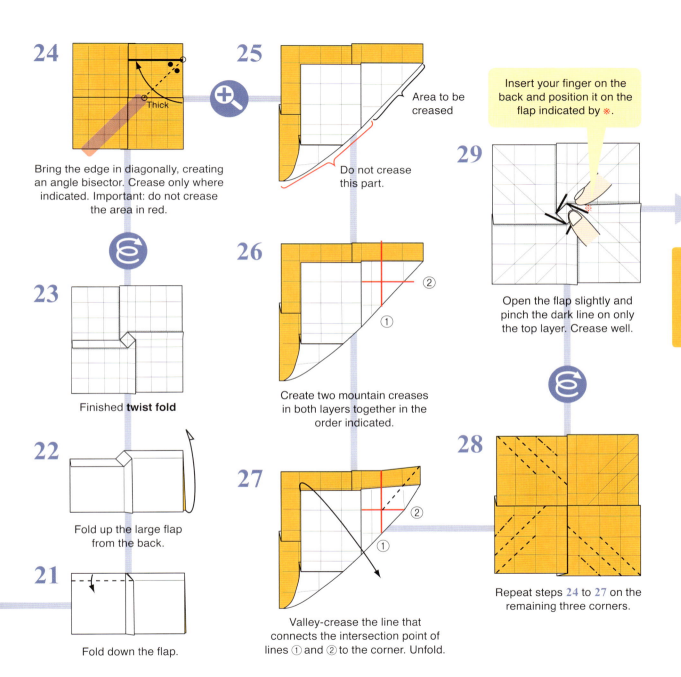

30

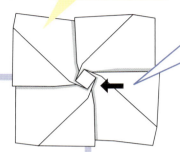

The center should naturally lift while the edges move down.

The creases that are not needed are not shown.

Note

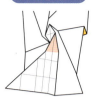

View from the direction that the arrow is pointing. The pink triangle becomes flat.

31

The center moves down, and the edges ★ move up.

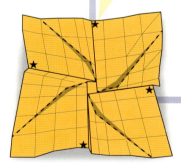

Make sure that the dashed lines are valley creases from edge to edge.

33

Repeat the previous step, alternating from the vertical to the horizontal flaps and pushing the paper gradually toward the center. The edges also move towards the center in a spiral shape.

32

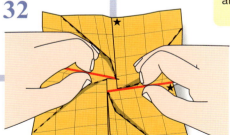

Pinch the red mountain creases using your thumbs and index fingers, and push down the valley crease using your middle fingers.

34

Three-dimensional Twist Fold

 View from the side

35

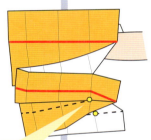

Bring the ○ points indicated together and valley-fold.

With one finger at the back of the red line, with your other hand reinforce the mountain crease, creating a prism.

36

Using a pen or similar tool, round the center to shape the internal petals.

40

Practice for steps 39 to 42

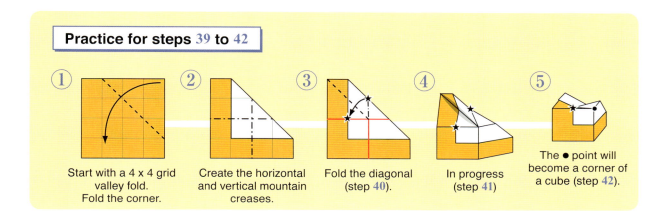

① Start with a 4 x 4 grid valley fold. Fold the corner.
② Create the horizontal and vertical mountain creases.
③ Fold the diagonal (step 40).
④ In progress (step 41)
⑤ The ● point will become a corner of a cube (step 42).

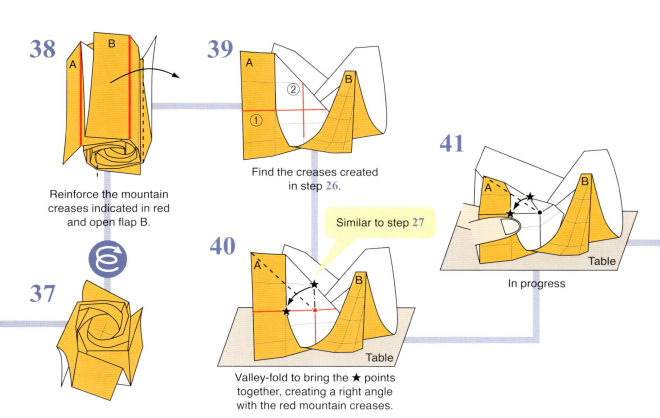

38 Reinforce the mountain creases indicated in red and open flap B.

39 Find the creases created in step 26.

40 Valley-fold to bring the ★ points together, creating a right angle with the red mountain creases. Similar to step 27.

41 In progress

37

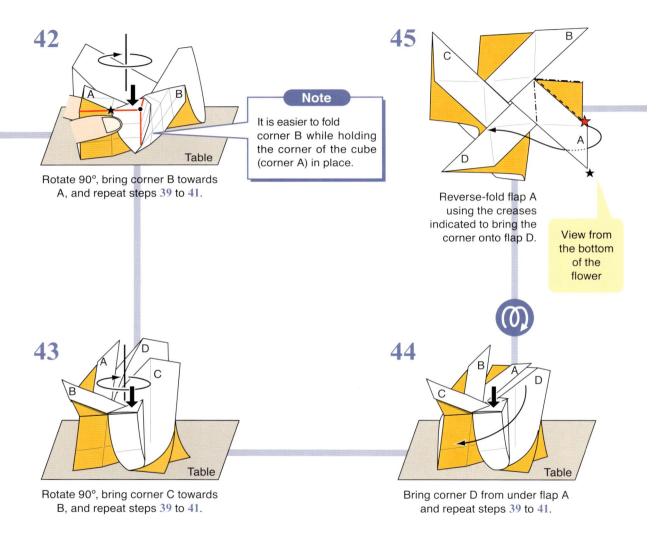

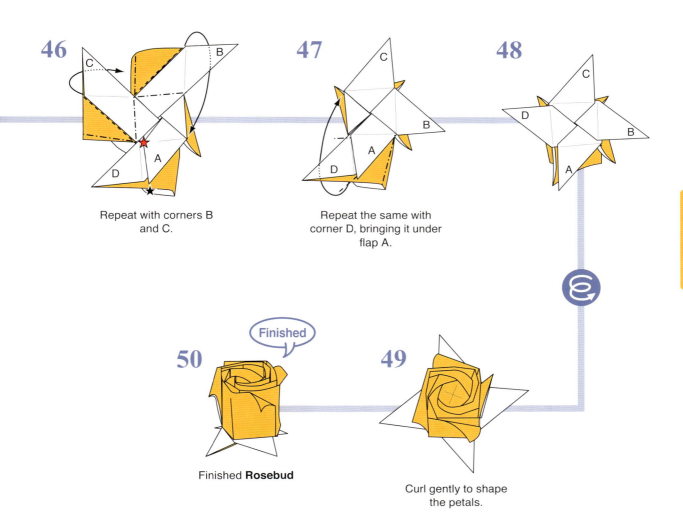

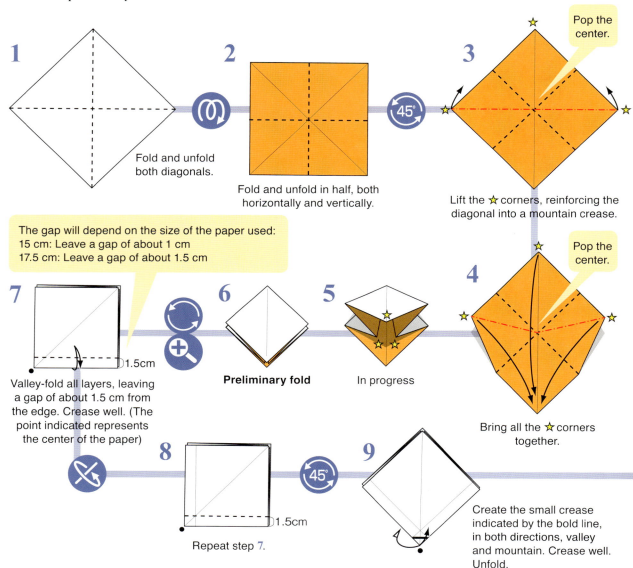

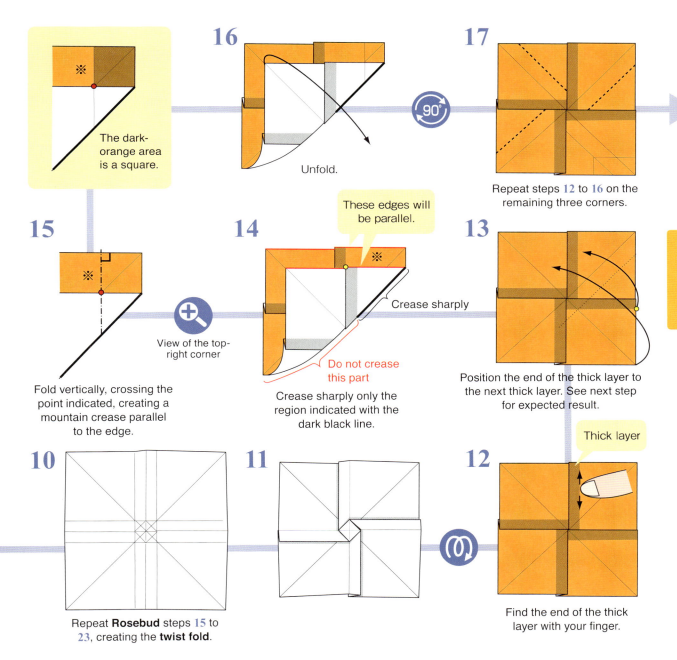

18

Position your finger under the ✻ point indicated.

19

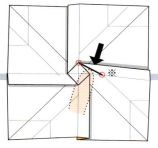

Push with the other finger as indicated by the arrow. Create a mountain crease on the bold line.

20

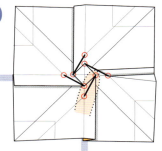

Repeat the previous steps on the remaining three corners.

22

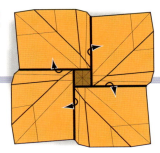

Stand the flaps up and use your fingernails to crease sharply the dark lines, making the model three-dimensional.

21

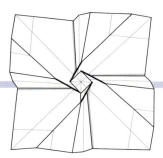

23

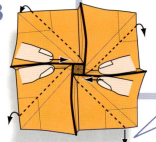

Holding the opposite flaps and pushing towards the center, allow the model to gently rotate clockwise.

Note

Move down the dashed lines.

24

Repeat step **23**, alternating between the vertical and horizontal flaps so that the complete model gradually turns into a spiral.

Perspective view

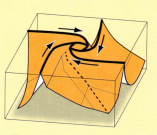

The dark crease lines are all at the same height.

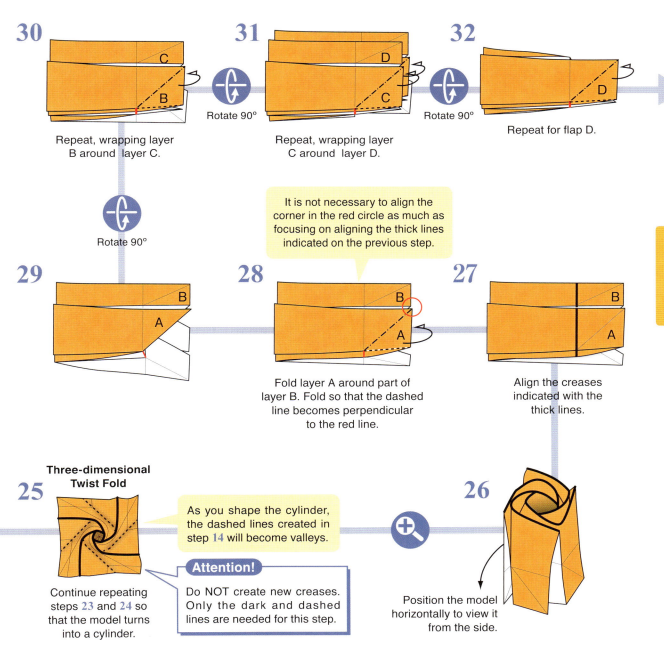

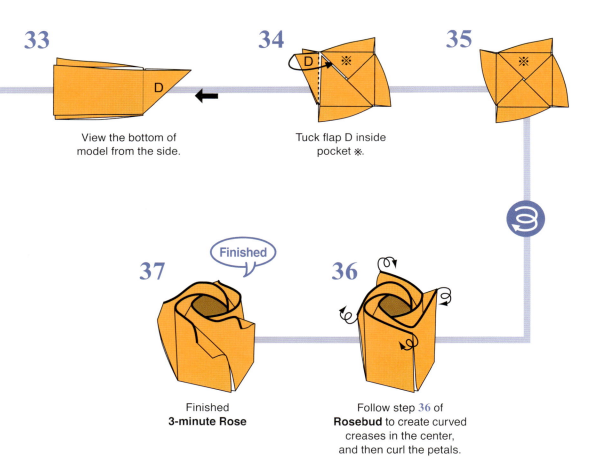

1-minute Rose

I often fold this Rose as a gift for people I happen to meet, getting them to choose their favorite color from the pack of Tant origami paper that I always carry with me. In particular, I like to give this Rose to restaurant chefs so that next time he remembers Kawasaki, the Origami Rose guy. Giving Roses also helps me to make friends with other customers sitting nearby. The "Kawasaki Rose" thus works like a business card. Because I can fold this model in a minute, I call it the 1-minute Rose.

Difficulty level ★★

1-minute Rose, 3-minute Rose, Rose Leaf

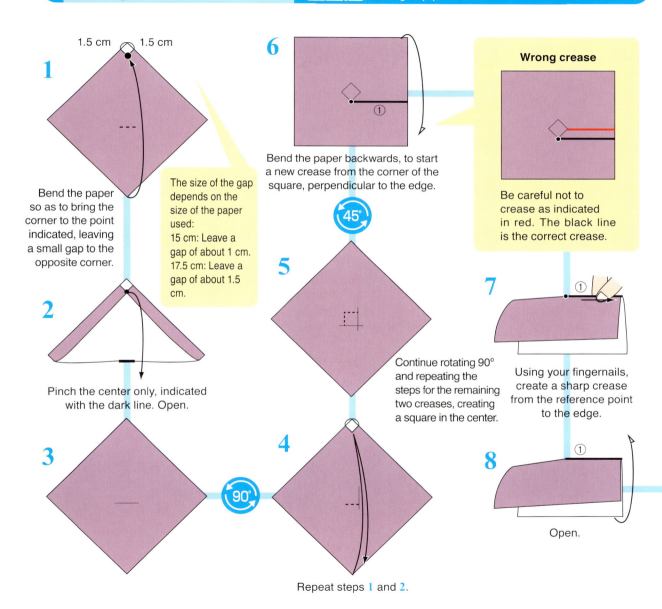

9

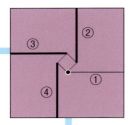

Repeat steps 6 to 8 on the remaining three edges.

14

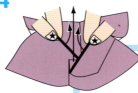

Holding the points indicated, move the center up as indicated.

Detail of the movement needed for step 14, indicated by the thick lines

The space between the ★ points does not change. The movement is based on the lines that rotate.

10

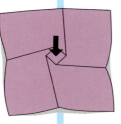

Pop the center to make the paper concave.

13

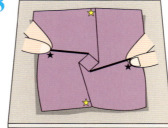

Place the square at the center of the paper on the surface of the table and lift the edges indicated.

15

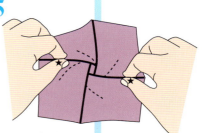

Verify that the valley creases (indicated by dashed lines) will naturally be created.

11

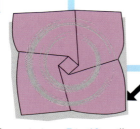

Repeat steps 7 to 10 until you obtain a three-dimensional shape that spins freely on top of the table.

12

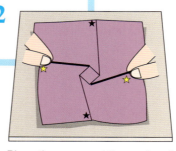

Place the square at the center of the paper on the surface of the table and lift the edges indicated.

16

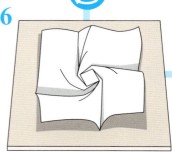

The edges indicated by the dark lines in step 15 create a plane that can be placed flat on the surface of the table.

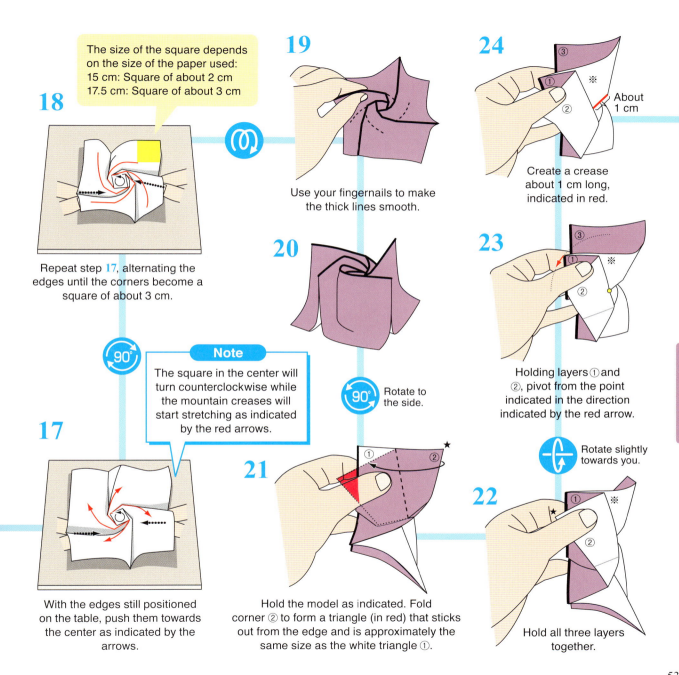

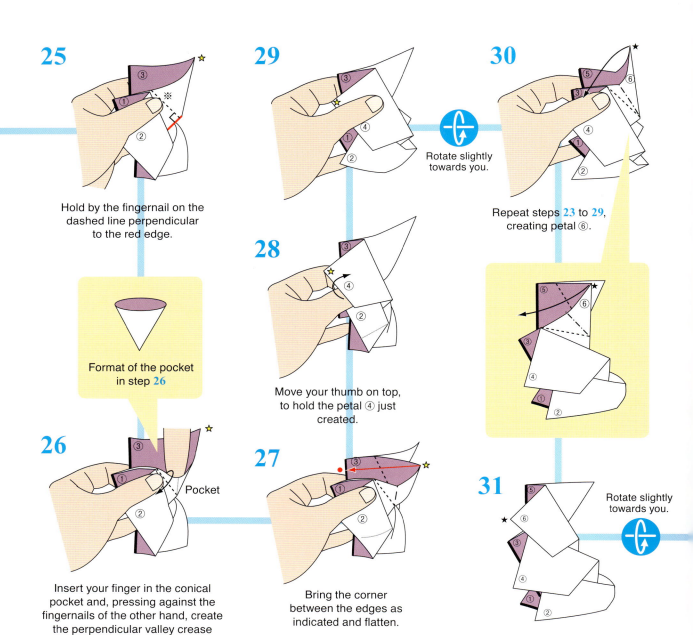

33

34

Once petal ② is squashed, position it back to the original position, under petal ④.

Rotate slightly towards you.

Move petal ② out from underneath petal ④ and repeat steps **23** to **29**.

38

View from the side.

37

Fold "c" and "d" inside, creating a circular base.

32

Repeat steps **23** to **29**, squashing to create petal ⑧.

Attention!
If the mountain fold is too narrow, the lock will not work well.

35

Imagine a line connecting the vertexes of the yellow triangles. Mountain-fold triangle "a" inside.

36

Repeat step **35** and fold triangle "b" inside.

1-minute Rose

55

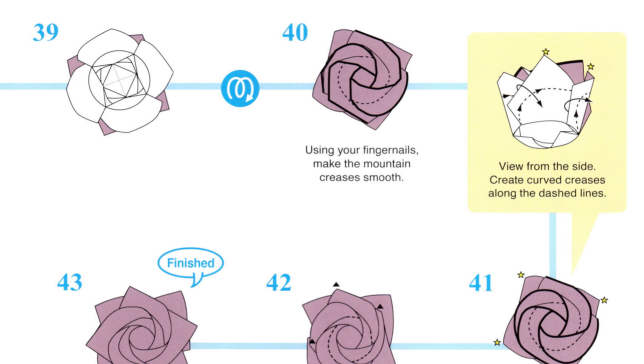

Rose

This is the model that is closest to a real rose. Because many special techniques are utilized, it is recommended that you practice the Rosebud before attempting this model. A fine grid is used to allow folding multiple petals. Because the finished model will be much smaller than the original paper used, it is recommended that you use a practice paper larger than 24 cm. The slanted grid should be creased as sharply and precisely as possible for a good final result.

Difficulty level ★★★

- Rose, Rose Leaf

Folding the Rose

Recommended paper size 17.5 cm - 30 cm square
Paper type Thin duo paper or washi paper

1 Bring opposite corner to opposite corner, creating creases of about 1-3 cm in the center of the paper.

2 Pivot the edges from the corner to the crease line.

3 ✗ ○ Be sure to create precise folds. Precise folds are the key to creating a beautiful model.

4 Fold edge to edge. Rotate.

5 Unfold.

6

7 Repeat steps **2** to **5** in the other direction.

8

9 Taking care not to let the paper drift, fold edge to edge.

10 Valley-fold all layers edge to edge. Be sure not to let the paper drift.

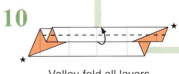

Rose

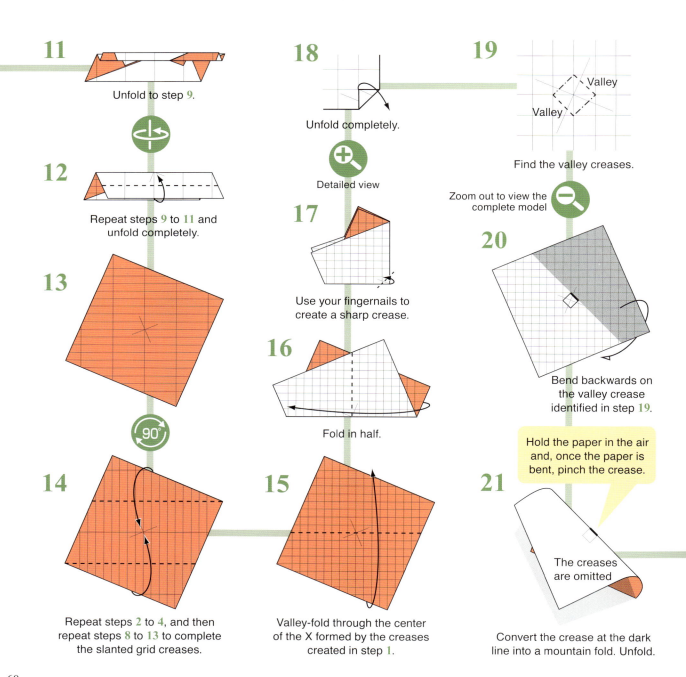

23

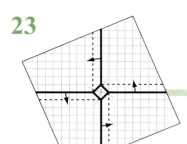

Create a **twist fold**, repeating steps **15** to **23** on pages 38 to 39.

24

Using substeps ① to ③, create a mountain crease between the points indicated.

①

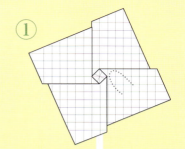

Position your finger inside, under the pleat.

②

Detailed view

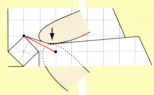

Pinch with your finger on top, flattening the flap.

③

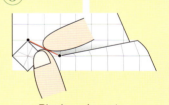

Pinch and create a mountain crease indicated by the red line.

22

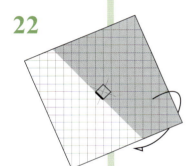

Repeat step **20** to convert the dark line into a mountain fold.

25

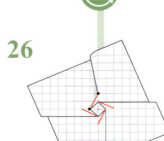

26

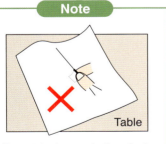

Repeat on the remaining three sides.

Note

Do not try to create the pinch with the model on the table.

Rose

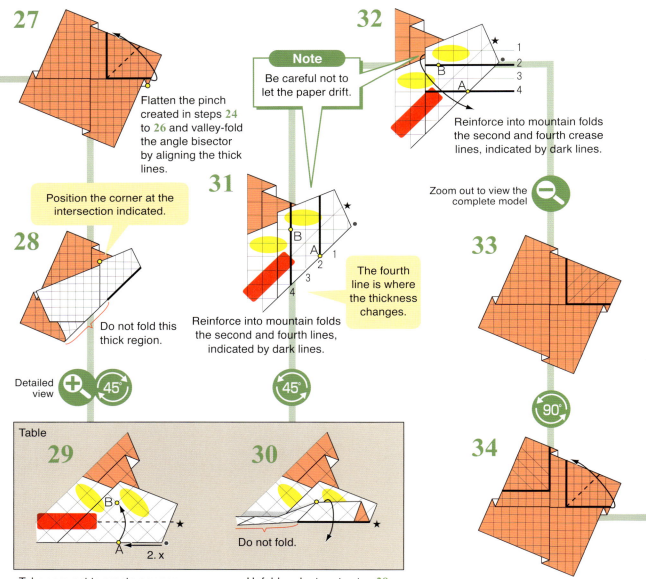

37

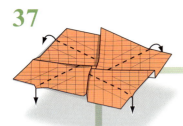

As with the **Rosebud**, stand the flaps up and bring the sides down on the valley creases, allowing the model to naturally turn into a spiral cylindrical shape.

36

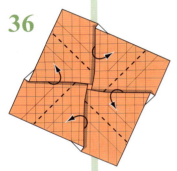

Make the flaps stand up.

35

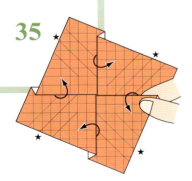

Make the flaps stand up.

In case you can't obtain the result shown in step **38**, practice the **Rosebud** steps **31** to **34**.

38

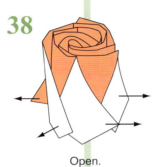

Open.

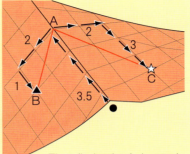

First, find point A, located 3.5 lines from the edge. On the left of A, point B can be found 2 lines to the left and 1 line towards the edge. Finally, point C is 2 lines to the right of A and 3 lines towards the edge.

39

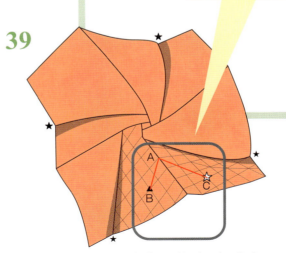

As indicated in the detailed view above, count the grid lines to find points A, B and C.

40

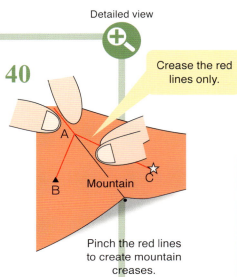

Detailed view

Crease the red lines only.

Pinch the red lines to create mountain creases.

41

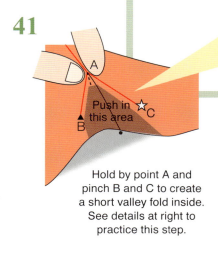

Hold by point A and pinch B and C to create a short valley fold inside. See details at right to practice this step.

Practice for step 41

The short valley fold for step 41 is equivalent to crease "c" in step ④ of this practice session.

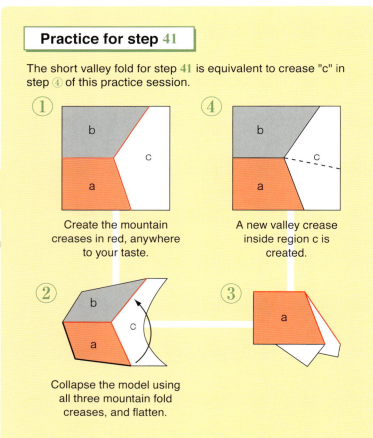

① Create the mountain creases in red, anywhere to your taste.

② Collapse the model using all three mountain fold creases, and flatten.

③

④ A new valley crease inside region c is created.

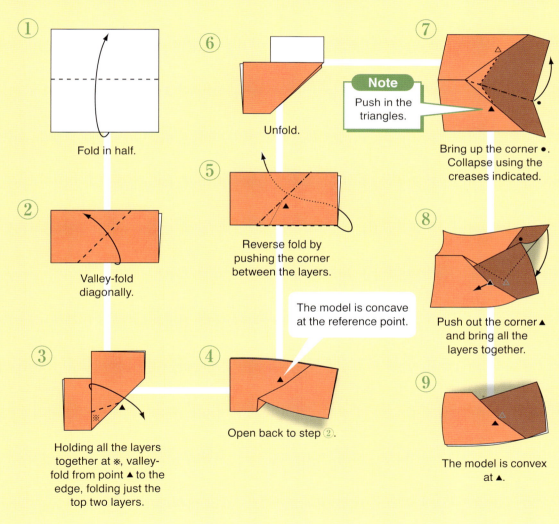

For steps **42** to **46**, refer to the practice steps described on the previous page.

42

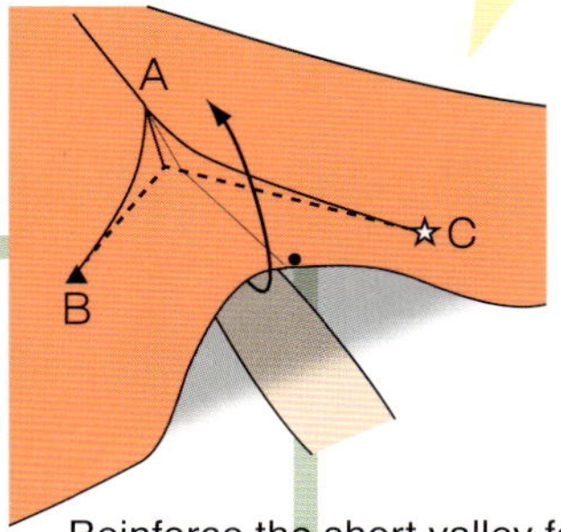

Reinforce the short valley fold created in the previous step, and create mountain creases AB and AC. Supporting the back of the paper with your finger, create new valley folds connecting the end of the short valley crease and points B and C.

43

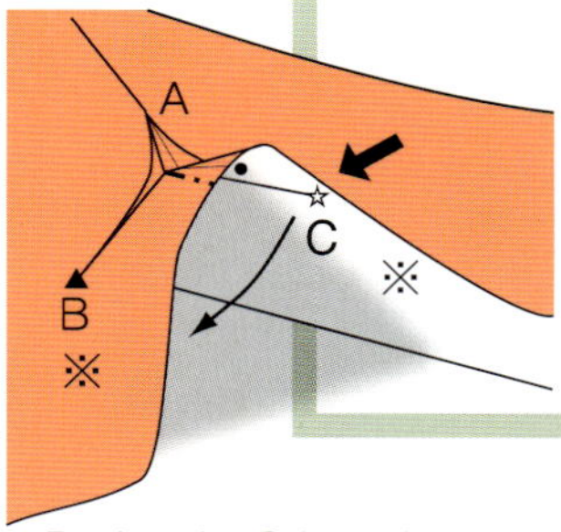

Push point C from the back as indicated by the arrow and bring the layers ※ together.

44

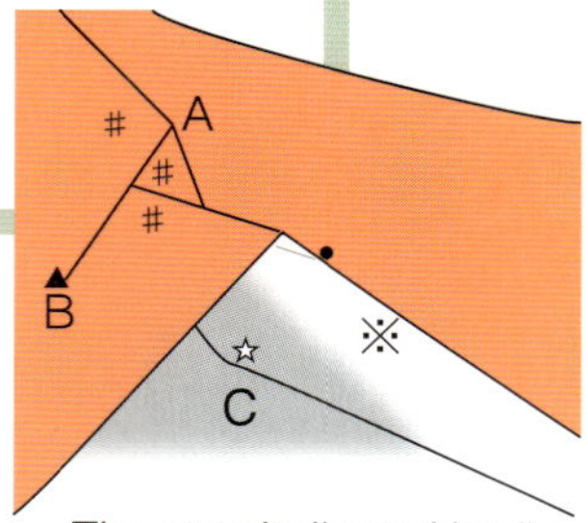

The area indicated by # will flatten. And both ▲ and ☆ should become convex.

Zoom out to view the complete model

45

Bring # to ※.

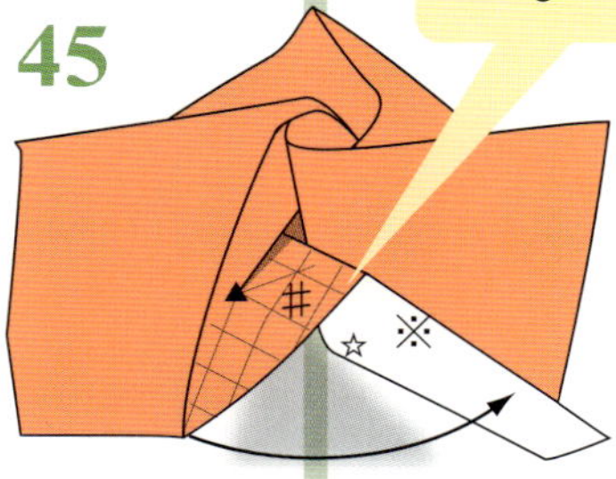

Bring the layers together.

46

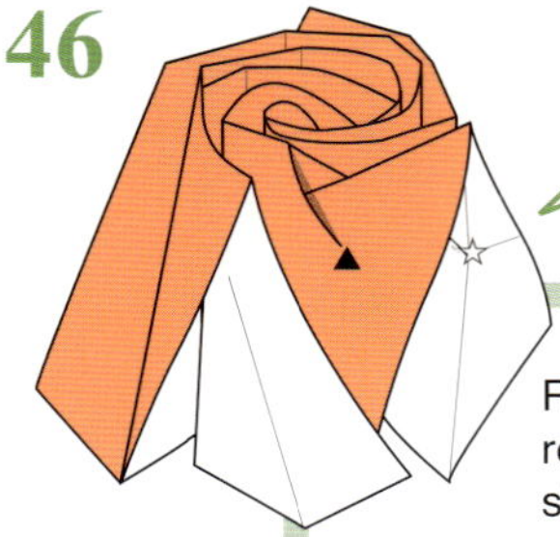

Attention!

Unlike in the "Practice for steps 42 to 46", points ▲ and ☆ will not overlap.

Repeat steps **40** to **46** on the remaining three petals, and shape in the same way as in step **38**.

47

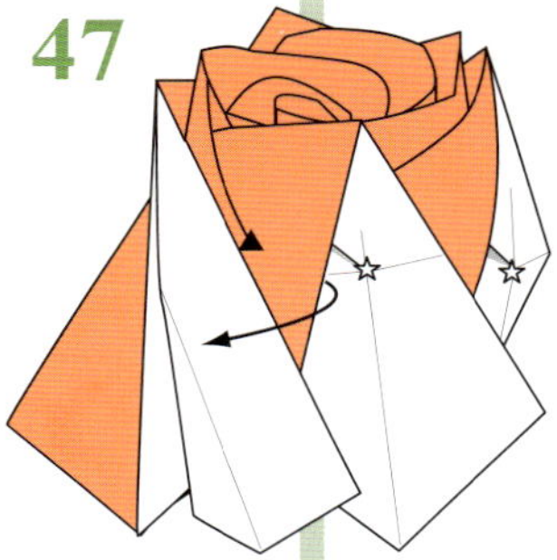

Loosen up the layers.

48

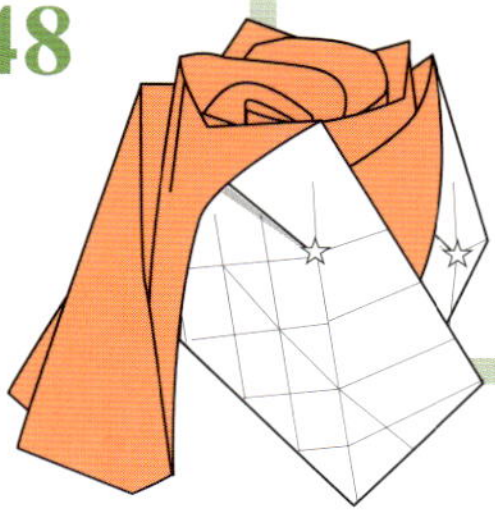

Check the grid creases.

Practice for step 49

① Mountain-fold corner to the back.

② Make the dark line into a mountain crease.

③ Bring the red lines together, creating a valley fold in the middle.

④ In progress

⑤ Cube corner. Open.

⑥

51 Locate the vertex of the cube corner and the reference point ☆ on the next flap.

Place the model on the table.

50

49

Very important! Hold the layer below together and do not let the paper drift.

Following the steps in the practice details above, fold the gray area in half and create a cube corner.

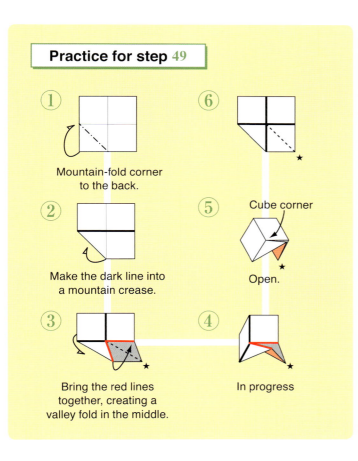
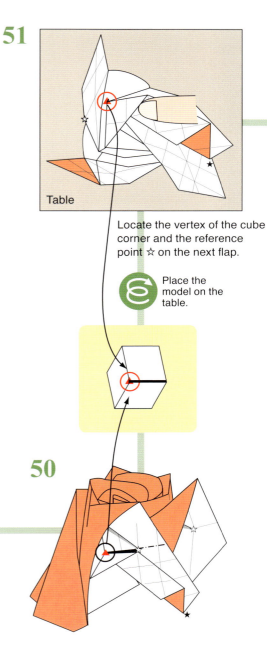
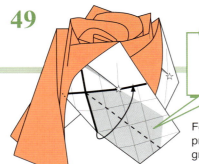

Rose

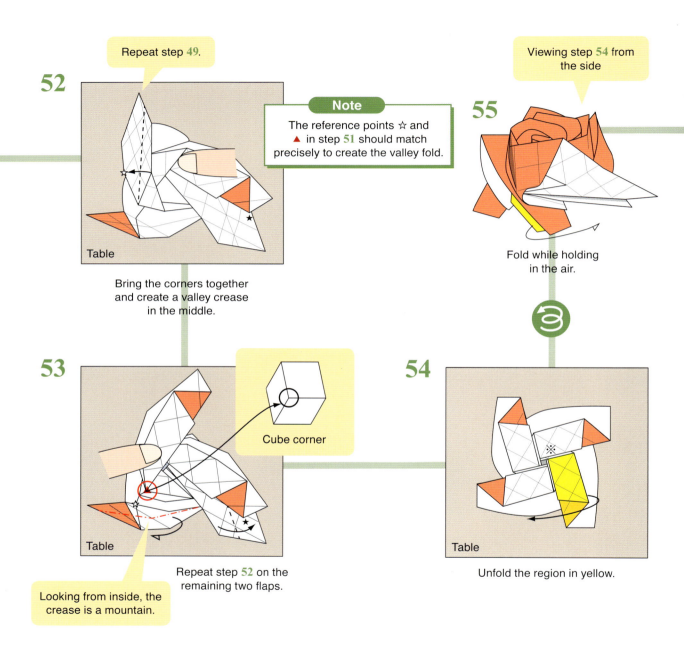

56

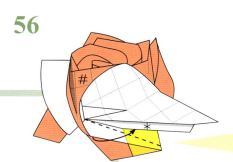

Valley-fold on the dashed line and tuck under the layer that is sagging.

56a

Valley-fold the edge and squash the small triangle shown in step **56b**.

Slightly off from the corner

56b

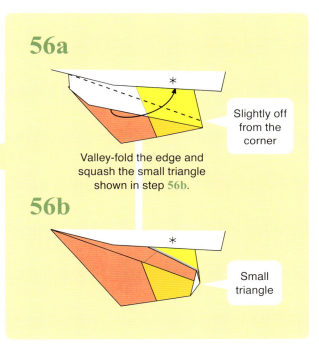

Small triangle

57

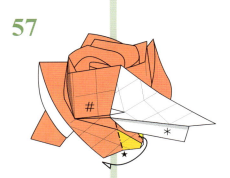

Fold backwards in the same way as in step **49**.

58

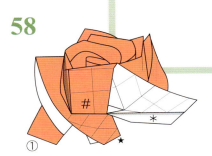

The layer # is no longer sagging as shown in step **56**.

Rotate 90°

59

Flaps ③ and ④ are hidden on the back of the model.

Repeat step **56** on the flaps following the order indicated.

Rose

69

60

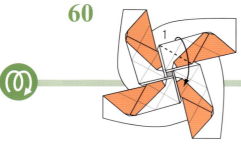

Make a **three-dimensional outside reverse fold**.

61

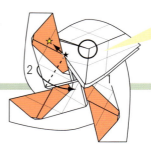

The ☆ is the corner underneath.

Shift the flap slightly (★ to ☆) before executing the **three-dimensional outside reverse fold**.

Practice for step 60: three-dimensional outside reverse fold

For this practice session, prepare a regular origami paper by cutting it in half.

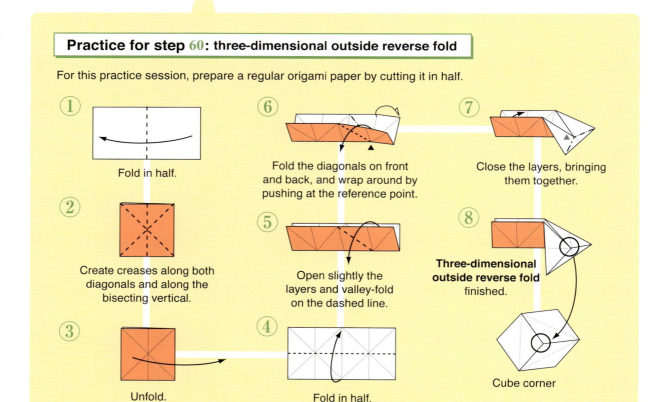

① Fold in half.

② Create creases along both diagonals and along the bisecting vertical.

③ Unfold.

④ Fold in half.

⑤ Open slightly the layers and valley-fold on the dashed line.

⑥ Fold the diagonals on front and back, and wrap around by pushing at the reference point.

⑦ Close the layers, bringing them together.

⑧ **Three-dimensional outside reverse fold** finished.

Cube corner

62
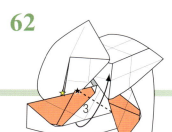
Repeat the **three-dimensional outside reverse fold**.

63
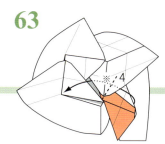
Make a **three-dimensional outside reverse fold** underneath ※.

64
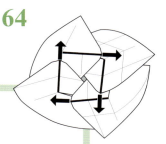
Adjust the dark mountain creases by pushing the edges in the directions indicated by the arrows. This should tighten the layers, creating a square base.

67
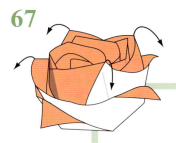
Curl the petals in the middle.

66

Curl the outside petals by creating curved creases.

65
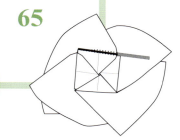
Use a toothpick under the edge to create a sharp mountain crease. Repeat on the other three edges.

68

Gently curve the inner petals.

69

Use a tool to shape the petals.

Make circular motions. Imagine grinding sesame seeds in a bowl.

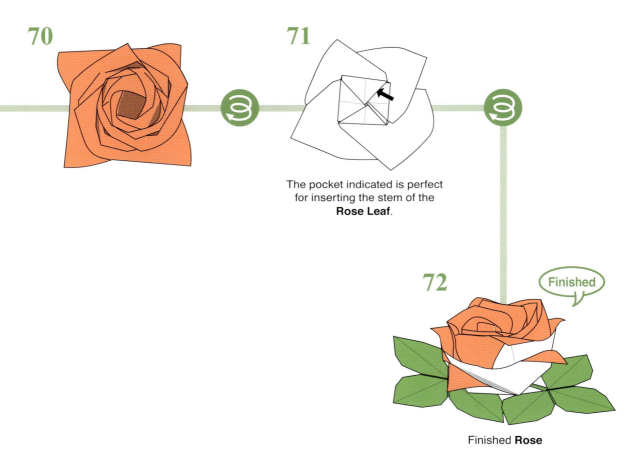

70

71
The pocket indicated is perfect for inserting the stem of the **Rose Leaf**.

72

Finished

Finished **Rose**

Heptagonal Rose Box

Conventional origami boxes are mostly modular, with three to six sides. My Heptagonal Rose Box, as the name implies, has a heptagonal base and can be folded with a single rectangular sheet. Using the new helical fold technique created in 2013, in which the paper is divided into isosceles triangles, you can create polygonal shapes not possible with the former helical fold: triangular, pentagonal, heptagonal. Scoring the paper with a ballpoint pen without ink or with a craft stylus will help create a better finish.

Difficulty level ★

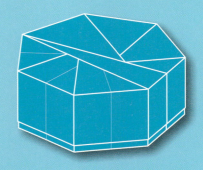

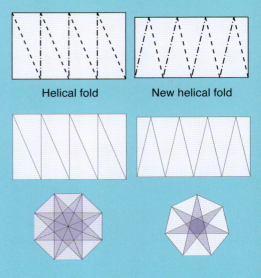

Helical fold   New helical fold

Heptagonal Box, Rose, Kawasaki Rose (Blossomed Rose),
1-minute Rose, Rosebud, Leaf with 3 Leaflets

Stage ▶ 1 Heptagonal Box

Recommended paper size: A4 (21 cm X 29.7 cm)
Paper type: Copy paper for practice; Construction paper for the final version.

1 A4 — W

Fold in half and unfold to create a crease in the middle.

2 D = W X 0.274

D, D, W

3 Calculate distance D, using the formula. For an A4 paper, that would be 5.75 cm. Using a pen without ink or a craft stylus, score the crease (mountain crease).

Crease in quarters.

4 Crease in eighths below the crease line.

5 0.5 mm below the crease — Exactly on the crease

Fold the edge to the line in red (notice the gap on the left side).

6 Unfold.

7 0.5 mm below the crease — Exactly on the crease

Repeat steps **5** to **6**.

8 Use a pen without ink or a craft stylus to score the valley creases.

9 Repeat step **8**.

Heptagonal Rose Box

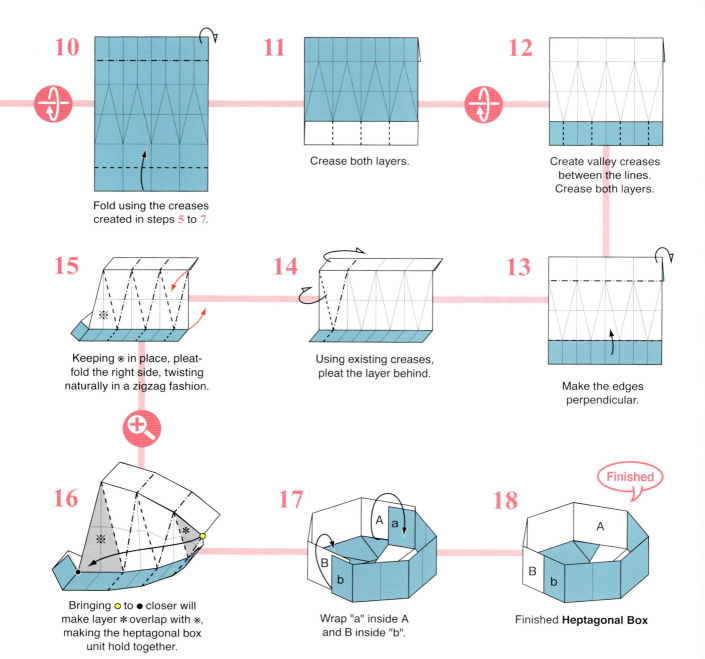

Stage ▶ 2 Heptagonal Rose Box

Recommended paper size: A4 (21 cm X 29.7 cm)
Paper type: Copy paper for practice; Construction paper for the final version.

The **Heptagonal Rose Box** is the Heptagonal Box with a lid. The difference between the lid and the box is the size of paper used. The folding sequence is the same as for the Heptagonal Box. The paper for the box is narrower and taller than for the lid, resulting in a deeper unit with a smaller diameter.

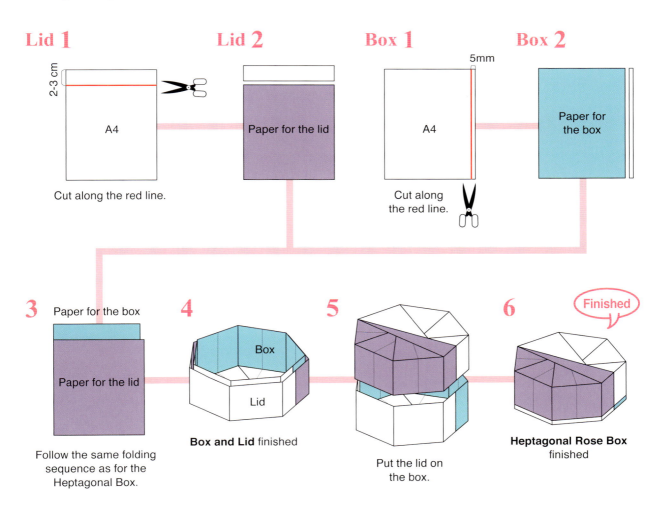

Paper used for the models in the photographs

Page	Model Name	Generic Name / Product Name <Vendor Name>
Cover	Rose	2 sheets of Tengujoshi washi paper glued together, High Class Origami Paper <Ehime Shiko> (Orange)
	Kawasaki Rose (Blossomed Rose)	Aiai Color <Ehime Shiko> (Vermilion)
	Kawasaki Rose (Bud)	High Class Origami Paper <Ehime Shiko> (Red)
	1-minute Rose	Tant (N50)
	Rose Leaf	Washi paper
p. 12	Kawasaki Rose (Bud)	Washi paper
p. 24	Rose	2 sheets of Tengujoshi washi paper glued together
	5-leaflet Leaf	Washi paper
p. 36	Rosebud	Washi paper (Red and Green glued back to back)
	Rose	Handmade washi paper (by Yukio Hamada, Living National Treasure of Japan), handmade washi paper, Ogawa washi (pink)
	3-leaflet Leaf	Handmade washi paper.
p. 50	1-minute Rose	Tant (N50)
	3-minute Rose	Tant (H50)
	Rose Leaf	Atsu kozo mura-zome washi paper, Aiai Color <Ehime Shiko> (Viridian)
p. 58	Rose	2 sheets of Tengujoshi washi paper glued together
	Rose Leaf	Washi paper
p. 74	Heptagonal Box	Construction paper
	Rose	High Class Origami Paper <Ehime Shiko> (Orange)
	Kawasaki Rose (Blossomed Rose)	Aiai Color <Ehime Shiko> (Sunflower)
	1-minute Rose	Tant (N57)
	Rosebud	Double-sided Origami Paper <Ehime Shiko> (Yellow Orange/Bright Green)
	3-leaflet Leaf	Aiai Color <Ehime Shiko> (Green)

TOSHIKAZU KAWASAKI is an origami artist and professor at the National Institute of Technology, Anan College. He was born in 1955. After entering university, he started creating his own origami models, characterized by an ingenious design style. His rose, in particular, known as the "Kawasaki Rose", is recognized worldwide. He received his PhD in number science, presenting a thesis on origami titled "Theory of Deformated Bird Bases". He is a leading expert in the field of mathematical origami research.

Rose Dream Origami

2016年10月5日　初版第1刷発行
著者　川崎敏和
訳者　野口マルシオ
協力　トーハン（ほんをうえるプロジェクト）
発行者　原 雅久
発行所　株式会社 朝日出版社
　　　　〒101-0065　東京都千代田区西神田3-3-5
　　　　電話　03-3263-3321（代表）
　　　　http://www.asahipress.com/
印刷・製本　図書印刷株式会社

Copyright ©2016 by Toshikazu Kawasaki
ISBN978-4-255-00941-4 C0076　Printed in Japan